FOR ALL OF US, ONE TODAY

FOR ALL OF US, ONE TODAY

An Inaugural Poet's Journey

Richard Blanco

BEACON PRESS, BOSTON

Beacon Press
www.beacon.org

Beacon Press books
are published under the auspices of
the Unitarian Universalist Association of Congregations.

16 15 14 13   8 7 6 5 4 3 2 1

This book is printed on acid-free paper that meets the uncoated paper
ANSI/NISO specifications for permanence as revised in 1992.

"América" from *City of a Hundred Fires* by Richard Blanco, © 1998.
Reprinted by permission of the University of Pittsburgh Press.

Text design and composition by Wilsted & Taylor Publishing Services
Translations by Gabriela Jauregui
Cover and interior art © Sergio Baradat

Library of Congress Cataloging-in-Publication Data
Blanco, Richard, 1968–
For all of us, one today : an inaugural poet's journey / Richard Blanco.
pages cm
ISBN 978-0-8070-3380-7 (pbk. : acid-free paper)—
ISBN 978-0-8070-3381-4 (ebook) (print)
1. Blanco, Richard, 1968– 2. Poets, American—Biography.
3. Immigrants—United States—Biography.
4. Gay men—United States—Biography. I. Title.
PS3552.L36533Z46 2013
811'.54—dc23
[B]   2013038547

FOR ALL OF US

from every walk of life doing what we do,
making what we make, loving who we love,
giving what we give, thanking what we're given,
praising what we believe, fighting what we fear,
wanting what we want, speaking how we speak,
and the telling of the stories we tell one another:
each of us shaping, evolving, reaching for the ideal
of this great experiment that is *we the people*,
that is our country with the word *hope*
as fresh on our tongues as it ever was.

One sun rose on us today . . .

D AYS BEFORE OUR FIELD TRIP TO THE SCIENCE
center, Mrs. Bermudez tells our class the sun is ac-
tually hundreds of times larger than the earth. *We move
around it. We're nothing, zooming through dark space*, she says,
matter-of-factly, as if it didn't matter that we were no lon-
ger the center of our own little worlds. *We*, with crayons in
our hands coloring dittos of the sun and *our* nine planets.
We, at our desks but also helplessly zooming through cold,
empty space. I don't want to believe her; the sun is the size
of a sunflower, I insist. I draw lemon-yellow petals around
it and color its center sienna brown. The first time I see a
lion I am nine years old, my grandfather's hands holding
me back from the cage I want to open. I can still feel his
grip and the lion's eyes staring at me like tiny, amber plan-
ets behind bars, asking me to set him free. My first kiss was
under the shade of moonlit palms in Janet Carballo's back-
yard, exactly two days before the end of the school year.
But I'm still feeling the powdery skin behind her earlobes,
smelling her strawberry lip gloss and the orange blossoms

in the air already thick with summer. I never saw a comet until I was twenty-four, cupped in the darkness of the Everglades and the arms of a man I loved. It was past midnight on a Sunday, I remember; I didn't go to work the next day. I'm still sleeping with the mangroves and the ibis, under a masterpiece of stars. The comet's tail a brushstroke of pure, genius light.

These are more than memories. They are what lives—and relives—inside our bodies, in every cell and heartbeat. The undiscovered DNA of our souls imprinted with the minute details of those eternal moments that change our lives, our stories, forever. Sometimes they're subtle, sometimes dramatic, but we know nothing will ever be the same the instant we experience them. And quite often they are unexpected.

On the afternoon of December 12, while casually driving back to my home in Maine, I receive a phone call with the news that I have been chosen as inaugural poet. Bewildered, I first wonder if it could be some cruel joke a friend might be playing on me. *You mean like Robert Frost? Like Maya Angelou?* I ask, wanting confirmation that what I just heard is true. *Yes. Yes,* I'm told, as I keep driving down the interstate in a daze, trying to speak, trying to fathom what has just happened. But I know. My body knows it's the most important moment of my life as a poet, a day by which I will mark the rest of my life, the day I learned that I will be named the fifth poet ever in our history to be US Inaugural Poet.

I'm asked by the Presidential Inaugural Committee to write not one but *three* poems in three weeks. Quite a challenge. But before any apprehension or pressure sets in, the world I move through is transfixed by my jubilation

and astonishment: one by one the birches along the high-
way turn from silver to gold; the bare-branched oaks traced
with snow become perfectly balanced sculptures; and the
highway stretches right into the sun. I begin the poem
in my mind as I drive, musing over a flood of lines and
images.

But then I catch my eyes in the rearview mirror; it
becomes a portal into my past. In my reflection I see my
father holding my hand for the last time, as he is quietly
dying in the spare room of the house where he raised me.
His eyes blink forever once: *goodbye*; twice: *forgive me*; three
times: *I won't be back*. Gone, into the space beyond the sun
and stars. I think of him, my mother, my grandparents—
their courage and sacrifices, all their struggles and hard
work to make a better life in America for themselves and
for my brother and me. Overcome by a wave of immense
gratitude, I pull off the highway, step out of the car, and
sit on the shoulder, leaning against the car door. Looking
into the sky, the sun becomes a sunflower again. *This is be-
cause of them* . . . I keep thinking and repeating . . . *because
of them* . . . *all because of them* . . .

One light, waking up rooftops,

under each one, a story . . .

EVERY STORY BEGINS INSIDE A STORY THAT'S
already begun by others. Long before we take our
first breath, there's a plot well under way with characters
and a setting we did not choose but which were chosen for
us. My journey as inaugural poet began with that December phone call, literally; but figuratively, it began a long
time ago in another journey full of sorrow and loss that
would end with hope and triumph.

1968: My parents summon every bit of courage and decide to emigrate from Cuba, exiling themselves from the
only country they have ever known, uncertain if they'll
ever again walk into the homes where they were born, or
sit in the town square where they courted each other, or
share a *cafecito* with their lifelong neighbors. In my mother's case, her entire family is reduced to a handful of photographs, black-and-white hopes of someday reliving even
the simplest pleasures of her past: tasting her mother's *arroz con pollo*, gossiping with her five sisters, dancing with

her eldest brother who taught her how to mambo when she was five years old.

On a dizzying flight from Havana, my parents arrive to the frigid drizzle of Madrid in December: one suitcase and the equivalent of fifty cents; my older brother, six years old; my mother, seven months pregnant with me. They share a one-floor apartment—*un piso*—with two other families, eat at soup kitchens, and wear mended winter coats from thrift shops. Two months later I'm born in a hospital run by Catholic charities. At home, my mother lays me down in an open drawer padded with towels—my first crib. But not for long. Weeks later, we emigrate once more, to New York City, where my paternal grandparents (exiled through Mexico) wait for us along with other relatives. My first baby picture is for my green card. I'm forty-five days old, a character in a story who already belongs to three countries.

Turn the page to another chapter: four years later, after my parents have saved enough money, we move to Westchester, a Miami suburb at the fringe of the county, sprawling westward with neon-lit strip malls, new sidewalks, and rows of identical houses built overnight it seemed. Despite its very Anglo-Saxon name, Westchester is a close-knit community of Cuban exiles like my parents, dutifully making their way with one eye on the American Dream and the other, nostalgic eye looking back toward the homeland and the lives they have left behind.

We settle into the house my mother still lives in today: a modest duplex shadowed by royal palms and mango trees, amid mild winters and summer's glorious thunderstorms pelting our terra-cotta rooftop. The setting mimics my parents' lost island paradise—a constant backdrop that feeds hopes of someday returning to their *patria*, their mother country, exactly as they had left it, to find their lives exactly as they were before, and step back into *their* story.

However, it was a story *I* had not lived, a story I couldn't quite piece together from snippets of conversations at the dinner table about the palm-lined streets of the sugar-mill town where *we* were from, or from my grandmother's gossip at the beauty salon damning *la comunista* who "stole" her house in Hormiguero. Sometimes the story was a fairy tale from my grandfather's lips, missing the taste of those mystical tropical fruits I'd never seen and the magical scent of the night jasmine in the backyard of his home in Cuba. Sometimes it was a tragedy told through the letters my mother read out loud from relatives in Cuba telling us about the sick, the dying, the executed. And sometimes it was a picture-book story from photo albums smuggled out of the country that I would page through, looking for my resemblance in the black-and-white eyes and smiles of *my* dark-haired cousins, *my* barefoot uncles in tank tops, or *my* aunts in paper-thin housecoats. Their faces unfamiliar, even though they *were* family.

Family as distant as the American families I watched on TV, where elegant mothers spoke English and didn't work outside their homes furnished with plush velvet sofas and polished coffee tables. Unlike my mother, they had time to prepare brown-bag lunches and cook dinner every night wearing pearl chokers and pumps. A world where fathers came home from the office on time every day, smoked pipes, read the newspaper in their cardigans, and said, *I*

8

love you, son, every night. Neighborhoods with oak-lined streets, where children were never called *fatso* or *faggot* like me. No, they rode shiny brand-new bicycles or walked from school to homes with emerald hedges, doorbells, and double-door garages. This was how I understood America, from reruns of shows like *The Brady Bunch, Leave It to Beaver,* and *My Three Sons.* Having never traveled outside my culturally insular Westchester, surrounded by people just like us, I truly believed an America exactly like the one on TV existed. That fantasy was the *real* America in my mind. Westchester felt like a kind of cultural purgatory, a waiting place caught between the real-imagined America and the real-imagined Cuba, both stories part of one story that I wouldn't weave together until living through my experiences as inaugural poet and forging through the creative process of writing the inaugural poems.

My face, your face . . .

To this day, I don't know exactly how I was chosen as inaugural poet. I asked committee staff, but no one seemed to know the details. I had never met the president—I've never met any president. In fact, I believe I am the only inaugural poet in history who didn't have some kind of personal connection to the administration that chose him or her. This made my selection even more surprising, and the honor felt even greater, given the trust they had placed in me and my work without ever knowing me personally. However, after a while, I began fearing that the exact details of my selection might not be what I had imagined, so I preferred to simply cling (and still do) to my romantic musings: the president reading my books in the Oval Office, so completely absorbed by my work that he tells his chief of staff to hold all his calls, no matter who; or, perhaps, the president reading my poems at the dinner table to the whole family; or, dare I imagine, he and the First Lady snuggled together in bed, reading my love poems to each other and discussing them with delight.

Perhaps there might have been some political affinity that influenced my selection, despite the family lore that I was named after Richard Nixon. After all, I *did* fill a lot of "boxes": I was the youngest, first openly gay, first immigrant, and first Latino inaugural poet. And the list could go on and on with other *firsts* that weren't really highlighted: first engineer, first Floridian, first Mainer, first poet with bushy eyebrows—wait, I think Frost may have beat me on that one! Regardless, I can't help believing that I was selected based on the quality of my work, and that the president must've read my poems and been personally involved in my selection, especially since he is such a literary person and an accomplished writer himself. I also can't help thinking that he may have chosen me because he connected with my story as a child of exiles/immigrants in the same way that I've always connected with his story. Surely he must have had to navigate questions about cultural identity, his place in America, and the American Dream throughout his life, as I've had to do.

Questions like the ones I had to face on the first day of my first graduate creative writing course at Florida International University. After we read and discussed poems by Whitman, Frost, and Ginsberg, Professor Campbell McGrath announced our assignment: *Write a poem about America.* Eager yet anxious, I thought: *What do I know about America? What is America?* Sprawled on my bed that night (and every night that whole week), I continued asking questions that hadn't really surfaced until then: *Was I American? Was I Cuban? Both? Neither? Where did I come from? Where do I belong?* Finally, the day before the assignment was due,

I gave up. Or I should say, I gave in—surrendered to the emotional truth about *my* experience, the only America I knew. I set to paper a poem I titled in Spanish "América," narrating my childhood pleas for an authentic meal at Thanksgiving, or *San Giving*, as my mother still calls it, as in *San Pedro, San Ignacio,* or *San Cristóbal*—a whole different kind of feast day!

AMÉRICA

I.
Although *Tía* Miriam boasted she discovered
at least half a dozen uses for peanut butter—
topping for guava shells in syrup,
butter substitute for Cuban toast,
hair conditioner and relaxer—
Mamá never knew what to make
of the monthly five-pound jars
handed out by the immigration department
until my friend, Jeff, mentioned jelly.

II.
There was always pork though,
for every birthday and wedding,
whole ones on Christmas and New Year's Eve,
even on Thanksgiving day—pork,
fried, broiled, or crispy skin roasted—
as well as cauldrons of black beans,

fried plantain chips, and *yuca con mojito.*
These items required a special visit
to Antonio's *Mercado* on the corner of Eighth Street
where men in *guayaberas* stood in senate
blaming Kennedy for everything—*"Ese hijo de puta!"*
the bile of Cuban coffee and cigar residue
filling the creases of their wrinkled lips;
clinging to one another's lies of lost wealth,
ashamed and empty as hollow trees.

III.
By seven I had grown suspicious—we were still here.
Overheard conversations about returning
had grown wistful and less frequent.
I spoke English; my parents didn't.
We didn't live in a two-story house
with a maid or a wood-panel station wagon
nor vacation camping in Colorado.
None of the girls had hair of gold;
none of my brothers or cousins
were named Greg, Peter, or Marcia;
we were not the Brady Bunch.
None of the black and white characters
on Donna Reed or on the Dick Van Dyke Show
were named Guadalupe, Lázaro, or Mercedes.
Patty Duke's family wasn't like us either—
they didn't have pork on Thanksgiving,
they ate turkey with cranberry sauce;
they didn't have *yuca*, they had yams
like the dittos of Pilgrims I colored in class.

IV.
A week before Thanksgiving
I explained to my *abuelita*
about the Indians and the Mayflower,
how Lincoln set the slaves free;
I explained to my parents about
the purple mountain's majesty,
"one if by land, two if by sea,"
the cherry tree, the tea party,
the amber waves of grain,
the "masses yearning to be free,"
liberty and justice for all, until
finally they agreed:
this Thanksgiving we would have turkey,
as well as pork.

V.
Abuelita prepared the poor fowl
as if committing an act of treason,
faking her enthusiasm for my sake.
Mamá set a frozen pumpkin pie in the oven
and prepared candied yams following instructions
I translated from the marshmallow bag.
The table was arrayed with gladiolas,
the plattered turkey loomed at the center
on plastic silver from Woolworth's.
Everyone sat in green velvet chairs
we had upholstered with clear vinyl,
except *Tío* Carlos and Toti, seated
in the folding chairs from the Salvation Army.

I uttered a bilingual blessing
and the turkey was passed around
like a game of Russian Roulette.
"DRY," *Tío* Berto complained, and proceeded
to drown the lean slices with pork fat drippings
and cranberry jelly—*"esa mierda roja,"* he called it.
Faces fell when *Mamá* presented her ochre pie—
pumpkin was a home remedy for ulcers, not a dessert.
Tía María made three rounds of Cuban coffee
then *Abuelo* and Pepe cleared the living room furniture,
put on a Celia Cruz LP and the entire family
began to *merengue* over the linoleum of our apartment,
sweating rum and coffee until they remembered—
it was 1970 and 46 degrees—
in *América.*
After repositioning the furniture,
an appropriate darkness filled the room.
Tío Berto was the last to leave.

Though I knew the poem was honest, I was unsure of it on many levels and apprehensive that it wouldn't measure up. However, much to my surprise and delight, the poem was met with tremendous praise and warmhearted laughter from my classmates and Professor McGrath in workshop. The reaction triggered something incredibly new for me emotionally and artistically. For years I had practically rejected my culture (to be of one mind with my parents' and grandparents' story just wasn't *cool* for a teenager). But after writing "América," I realized their story of exile/immigration was as much mine as it was theirs, albeit a story I didn't know exactly but was suddenly compelled to discover through poetry. "América" eventually became the opening poem in my first book, *City of a Hundred Fires*, titled after the Cuban city of Cienfuegos, where my parents were from. Reaching back into my life, into *my* story within *their* story, and negotiating a cultural identity became the driving tension and theme of two subsequent collections of poetry, several essays I would write over the next twelve years, and even the inaugural poems.

. . . so I could write this poem . . .

HOW DID I COME TO POETRY IN THE FIRST PLACE? Well, I'm not one of those poets who claims to have been writing poems since I was in the womb. However, I have been possessed by a creative spirit and curiosity since I was a child, taking great pride in my Mickey Mouse coloring books, my Lego houses, and my Play-Doh sculptures. On the other hand, I was also a whiz at math and the sciences. Truly a left-brained, right-brained person, I scored exactly the same on the analytical and verbal sections of every standardized test I ever took. But we were a relatively poor working-class family simply trying to survive; the arts were certainly not dinner conversation. What's more, there was a cultural divide: my parents didn't even know who the Rolling Stones or Mary Tyler Moore were, for example, much less Robert Frost. That was part of the story I was born into and the reason why a life in the arts was just outside the realm of possibility. Like many immigrants, my parents strongly encouraged me to pursue a sound, financially rewarding career to ensure I'd have a *better life* than they had had. So, on the advice of my father, I chose civil engineering, believing that someday, somehow I'd explore my *other* side, though I didn't imagine it would ever be through poetry.

After graduating with honors, I established my civil engineering career, making my family—and myself—proud. By my mid-twenties, however, I felt accomplished and confident enough to begin exploring those creative impulses that had lain dormant. I entertained thoughts of becoming a painter or applying to graduate school for architecture but never followed through. Nothing felt quite right. Nothing stuck.

Then the unexpected happened. In the course of my engineering duties at the offices of my employer, C3TS, I began writing inch-thick reports, proposals, and lengthy letters to clients and permitting agencies. Consequently, I started paying very close attention to the way language worked to organize my thoughts, argue a point, or create a persona, noticing the subtle yet important differences between writing "but" instead of "however" or "therefore" instead of "consequently." I discovered that language had to be *engineered* in a way, just like the bridges and roads I was designing. It had to be concise, accurate, effective, and precise—the same terms one might use to describe a poem.

Eventually I couldn't resist the urge to pick up a pen and explore writing for my own personal expression, merely as a creative outlet at first. My earliest poems weren't very good, but they weren't terrible either, according to the friends and former writing instructors with whom I shared my work. Somehow—perhaps because I felt I had nothing to lose—I was never bashful about showing my poems to others. Encouraged, the more I wrote and read poems, the more my fascination with language grew.

One night, while pondering "The Red Wheelbarrow" by William Carlos Williams, I noticed my mother in the kitchen preparing dinner and suddenly became aware of the violence of her hands chopping onions and bell peppers, the dull glint of that same old knife she'd used since I was a child, the faded tomato-sauce stains on her apron, and the smell of olive oil sizzling through the house. In that instant, time seemed to stop, and I grasped the power of imagery to transform the ordinary into the extraordinary, into poetry, into a poem where my mother was not *just* my mother and a wheelbarrow was not *just* a wheelbarrow.

It was another of those life-changing moments—the moment I *got* poetry as a real, living thing and decided to pursue the art more seriously, though with only a vague sense of what becoming a *real* poet meant. So I took the next step and enrolled in a series of creative writing courses at a community college in Miami. There I began formally understanding the discipline of the craft behind the magic of the art. And as I engaged with more seasoned poets, I became more seasoned and serious myself. Eventually I applied and was accepted to the master's program in creative writing at Florida International University, though I continued working full-time as an engineer. I graduated from the creative writing program the same year I passed my engineering board exam, meaning I got my poetic license and my engineering license at the same time!

Richard Blanco, PE, which stood for *Professional Engineer* as well as *Poet Engineer*, as I was playfully dubbed by my coworkers. In retrospect, I now consider the irony of how my cultural circumstances led me to engineering, yet engineering led me to write poetry that explored my cultural circumstances. Which came first: the engineer or the poet?

. . . the empty desks of twenty children . . .

SORTING OUT MY CULTURAL CONTRADICTIONS AND yearnings and what it meant, by contrast, to be—or not to be—an American became an obsession, the central themes of my poems since graduate school and to this day. I would say I had been writing about America long before I got the assignment from the Presidential Inaugural Committee. As such, at first I felt somewhat comfortable and cautiously confident about writing the inaugural poem. After all, it *was* the same assignment as the one from years before: *Write a poem about America*. Or so I thought.

Ready to work the very first day after I got the call, I relocated my laptop and printer from my office to the kitchen table downstairs, as I usually do whenever I tackle a big writing project. Changing my environment helps stimulate creativity, even if it means simply changing the view in the window from the pond at the front of our house to the saw-tooth profile of the White Mountains that grace the windows of my kitchen and living room. My dog, Joey, followed me downstairs, sleeping all day by the fireplace, as did my two cats, Buddha and Sammy, joining me at the table, their tails tick-tocking the minutes, then hours away as I stared at a blank screen.

I spent the next two days in a creative incubation period, reading and thinking about the assignment, its possibilities and potential pitfalls as I waited for the muse to strike. Naturally, I first turned to the inaugural poems by Robert Frost, Maya Angelou, Miller Williams, and Elizabeth Alexander, studying their respective approaches and how each fulfilled the assignment. Suddenly, in the company of such great poets, I felt part of a continuum, wanting to honor them with humility and grace by offering my voice, adding to the story they had told in their poems—the story of our country. I was entranced by Angelou's use of symbols—*the rock, the tree, the river*—as a form of shorthand that spoke through the power of nature, and impressed by Alexander's images and catalog of people going about their morning. I mused over the America represented in Frost's poem in contrast to the present-day America I had to speak to. All these elements would eventually influence the writing of "One Today."

For further inspiration, I turned to poets I had long admired for the emotional accessibility of their voices that spoke plain and true. Among these, some old favorites: Elizabeth Bishop, Robert Hass, Philip Levine, Pablo Neruda, Sandra Cisneros, Adam Zagajewski, Martín Espada, Billy Collins, and Campbell McGrath, my mentor and former professor. All these voices have been essential to the cultivation of my own voice throughout the years. I also paged through poems of some newer favorites who have touched my soul: Rachel McKibbens, Ada Limón, and Marlena Mörling. And I riffled through the *Norton Anthology of Modern Poetry* but was surprised to find so few poems (outside of Whitman's and Ginsberg's) that had taken on the subject of America with the breadth and scope I thought necessary for the occasion. Then again, I wasn't surprised: the occasional poem has never been front and center in American poetry. I came to accept the inaugural poem as its own genre, practically. But still, no breakthrough in the writing.

During the incubation period I also considered my many hats as the first gay, first immigrant, and first Latino inaugural poet, initially feeling a self-imposed pressure or temptation to write poems that would have some political charge. But I soon decided that my selection was enough of a statement. It would be redundant or much too obvious to write a poem that spoke directly to what I already represented as a person. And besides, my work has never been characterized as political. It would have been out of character—disingenuous—for me. *Leave the politics to the politicians—that's their genre, not mine*, I thought. I came to understand my role—the historical role of the inaugural poet—as visionary and the poem as a vision of what could be (celebratory, uplifting, hopeful), reaching for our highest aspirations as a country and a people. Yet I also knew I had to fold in some kind of tension and hard truth—not come across as a greeting-card poet. But, still, inspiration would not strike.

By the third day, anxiety really began to set in as I faced the reality of my assignment: three poems in three weeks, one of which would arguably be the most important poem of my writing life—and then having to read it to millions on the world stage! I started meditating daily, trying to let go of my apprehensions and surrender to the muse. I called upon my spiritual ancestors for help and guidance. And I worked through a lot of false starts and drafts of poems I chose to abandon. During mental breaks and at lunchtime, or at moments when I was at my wit's end and *had* to disconnect, I'd watch recorded episodes of *The Mary Tyler Moore Show*, *Bewitched*, and, my favorite, *The Brady Bunch*—as I always have, still addicted to that yesteryear version of America. Then the news of the shootings at Sandy Hook Elementary broke—another one of those moments I instantly knew would live inside me—inside us—forever.

Marcia Brady's maudlin tears over her broken nose against the tears on the speechless faces of parents who'd lost their children; Mary Tyler Moore's constant good cheer against President Obama's grief-stricken countenance during the memorial service; Samantha Stevens's perfect house in Connecticut and her magical powers against the powerless reality of Sandy Hook—all these sharp contrasts triggered a turning point in my connection with America and a creative breakthrough. Just days before I had spent an entire day with students at a middle school in Connecticut, reading and talking about poetry, lighting up the faces of children like the faces of the children at Sandy Hook. It affected me more than any other American tragedy in my lifetime. And I realized that, in addition to my parents' story, there was another story I had been born into—the story of America—one I had not yet fully explored or embraced in my writing or my life. Not the imaginary America on TV but the real, real American family I felt I belonged to through the Sandy Hook tragedy, those parents and children that our entire country wanted to hold and comfort. I knew then, without question, that I would do my best to honor and remember them forever in my inaugural poem.

The tragedy opened a new emotional and creative pathway for me. Writing the inaugural poem wasn't the *same* assignment anymore. I suddenly understood that as a Cuban-American, I hadn't explored my American side of the hyphen as much as my Cuban side. There had always been some small part of me that didn't really *feel* American. The true American boy seemed like someone else, not me exactly. Perhaps I had subscribed to the mindset of my exile community, which saw their lives here only as temporary; America was home, but not a permanent one. Just as my parents wanted to return to their island paradise, perhaps all along I had wanted to return to the paradise of that America I had idealized since grade school, though both were just as imaginary, just as unreachable. I began asking questions of myself and our country that I had never before dared to ask or explore. The three inaugural poems I would eventually write, including "One Today," were, in one way or another, inspired responses to those questions I asked myself.

One ground. Our ground . . .

*D*O I TRULY LOVE AMERICA? IT WAS A QUESTION I had to answer honestly if I was going to write an honest poem. I began thinking of my relationship with America and how it had evolved through different phases, just as my consciousness of love had evolved, especially with my partner, Mark. I saw parallels between a loving human relationship and the love we hold for our country. This was the genesis of the first poem, "What We Know of Country," which begins as young love begins, with a certain childlike innocence, the perception of the beloved— of country—as flawless. For me, that meant believing the fairy-tale version of Thanksgiving with the much-too-kind-hearted Pilgrims and their gold-buckled shoes, an obsession of mine since childhood, and recalling my fascination with "My country 'tis of thee" and the national anthem, thinking it addressed Latinos like us in the opening line: "O, José can you see . . ."

That innocence eventually expanded into a broader sense of nationality and community, a feeling of belonging to something larger, just as when love evolves from the *I* to the *we* and so forth through various stages of understanding, until the romantic illusions I had held about our country ruptured and I faced the historical truths, no longer looking at America through red-white-and-blue-colored lenses. But eventually, as with a relationship, there came a time to forgive and accept that neither love nor country is perfect. Through the process of writing "What We Know of Country," I discovered that *yes, I truly loved America*, but not with a blind love or blind patriotism. Rather, with a love that's much like loving another person, a love that demands effort, asks us to give and take and forgive and constantly examine promises spoken and unspoken.

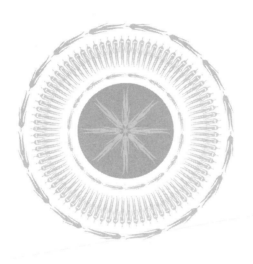

LO QUE SABEMOS
DE LA PATRIA

Acuérdate de esos libros de cuentos
de los días de primaria en los que los peregrinos llegaban
con sombreros altos y zapatos de hebillas doradas que morías
por tener, en los que hombres altos y erguidos en cuartos
con cortinas de terciopelo, con pelucas blancas, y plumas en mano
firmaban palabras que volaban como colibrís de la página
hasta el oído de tu corazón: *Life, Liberty, Happiness*
para *We, the people* cantando de mares resplandecientes
atravesados bajo cielos amplios a una tierra bendita cuando
lo que sabías de tu patria era sólo una canción y un libro.

Tal vez has olvidado la capital de Vermont
o Iowa, pero seguramente recuerdas tus ojos
en el mapa, memorizando ciudades y pueblos distantes
que casi no podías pronunciar; ni tampoco podías creer,
que esa inmensidad, esa tierra te pertenecía
y tu a ella: espina de las Rocosas, ojos azules

WHAT WE KNOW
OF COUNTRY

Let me take you back into those picture books
from grade school days where pilgrims landed
in tall hats and those gold-buckled shoes I wanted
so badly, where men in white wigs stood tall
in velvet-curtained rooms, feathers in their hands
inking words buzzing off the pages like hummingbirds
right into your heart's ear: *Life, Liberty, Happiness*
for *We, the people* singing of shining seas crossed
under spacious skies to a God-blessed land when
a song and a book was all we knew of country.

Maybe you forgot the capital of Vermont
or Iowa, but surely you remember your eyes
on the map memorizing far away cities and towns
you could hardly pronounce, nor scarcely believe
that vastness, that body of land that belonged to you,
and you to it: spine of the Rockies, blue eyes

de los Grandes Lagos, hombros de las costas infinitas,
las caderas de incontables puertos, ríos como las líneas
de tus palmas trazadas con asombro de principio
a fin, y el puntico de tu corazón marcaba
orgullosamente dónde vivías, cuando 'patria'
era eso que descubrías en un mapa.

Querías vivir en esa casa soñada, esa
que veías en la televisión: con sofás acolchonados
y bomboneras de cristal, donde las madres servían
pavos perfectamente rostizados con relleno instantáneo,
donde los niños tenían mesadas y dientes perfectos,
donde los padres manejaban autos con aletas plateadas
hasta aquel club al que seguramente pertenecerías
algún día. Los disparos y la sangre de las guerras
se oían hasta tu recámara, pero te dormías;
hombres de la luna aterrizaban en tu techo
con falsas promesas del espacio, pero la fantasía
era lo único que querías saber de la patria.

No querías cambiar el canal pero
lo hiciste, ¿te acuerdas? Abriste las persianas,
dejaste que la luz brillara sobre las alfombras cubiertas de
    mentiras
que no habías visto, notaste el polvo de secretos asentado
sobre las fotos, y la casa empezó a rechinar,
a derrumbarse a tu alrededor, mientras tú, sentado solo en la mesa
de la cocina durante años, el último en saber, le gritabas
a tu reflejo en las ventanas: *América, cómo*
pudiste?, sin ninguna respuesta imaginable,
pues todo lo que sabías de la patria era tu rabia.

of Great Lakes, shoulders of endless coastlines,
curvy hips of untold harbors, rivers like the lines
of your palms traced with wonder beginning
to end, and the tiny dot of your heart marking
proudly where you lived—when what we knew
of country was what we discovered on a map.

We all wanted to live in that house—the one
dreamed up on television with cushy sofas
and crystal candy dishes, where mothers served
perfectly roasted turkeys with instant stuffing,
where children had allowances and perfect teeth,
where fathers drove teal-blue cars with silver fins
to that country club you'd surely belong to
someday. The gunfire and blood of wars beamed
down into your bedroom, but you fell asleep;
men from the moon landed on your rooftop
with empty promises from space, but fantasy
was all we wanted to know of country.

You didn't want to change the channel, but
you did—remember? You parted the shades,
let light shine on the carpets stained with lies
you'd missed, saw the dust of secrets settled
over the photos, and the house began to creak,
slowly fall apart around you, alone for years
at the kitchen table, the last to know, shouting
at your reflection in the windows: *How could you,
America?* with no answer you could imagine
for all you knew of country was your rage.

Pero tu hogar era tu hogar, así que desempolvaste
los secretos, limpiaste las mentiras, y encendiste la chimenea.
Te sentaste con libros que nunca habías abierto,
escuchaste canciones que nunca habías tocado,
sacaste el viejo mapa de un cajón oscuro
y lo redibujaste con más colores y menos líneas.
Atizaste el fuego que seguía ardiendo hasta que, *Bueno,*
nada es perfecto, entendiste, *te perdono,*
dijiste—y el perdón se volvió tu patria.

Te quedaste, me quedé, nos quedamos todos por los muchachos
que regresaron como hombres, algunos sin
piernas; nos quedamos por la caída del Challenger y por las Torres
cuando se desmayaron del cielo; por los valientes
de Nueva Orleans varados en los techos como pájaros sin alas,
por el mar que se hinchó contra el norte hasta que
barrimos cada grano de arena de regreso a la orilla,
nos quedamos para encender veinte velas para veinte
niños, y tal vez sentir lo que siempre habíamos sentido:
conocer la patria requiere todo lo que sabemos del amor.

Algunos días mejor que otros, pero nunca fáciles:
cada mañana de cada año de cada siglo, nuestra promesa
de despertarnos y bajar los escalones con esperanza
rabiosa a sentarnos en la mesa de la cocina otra vez
con los ojos aún borrosos, aún cansados, y decir: *Mira,*
tenemos que hablar—eso es lo que sabemos de la patria.

But home was home, so you dusted off
the secrets, cleaned up the lies, nailed down
the creaky floor boards, and started a fire.
You sat with books you had never opened,
listened to the songs you had never played,
pulled out the old map from a dark drawer,
and redrew it with more colors, fewer lines.
You stoked the fire, burning on until finally *Okay,
nothing's perfect*, you understood, *I forgive you*,
you said—and forgiveness became your country.

You stayed, I stayed, we stayed for the boys
when they came back as men, some without
legs, for the fall of the Challenger and Towers
as they fainted from the sky, for the Big Easy's
brave stranded on rooftops like flightless birds,
for the sea that swelled against the north until
we swept every grain of sand back to shore,
for the lighting of twenty candles for twenty
children, feeling perhaps what we've always felt:
to know a country takes all we know of love.

Some days better than others, but never easy:
every morning of every year, of every century
our promise to wake up, stumble downstairs
with our raging hope, sit at the kitchen table
again, still blurry-eyed, still tired, and say: *Listen,
we need to talk*—that's what we know of country.

. . . some days giving thanks for a love

that loves you back . . .

I N THE WAY "WHAT WE KNOW OF COUNTRY" SPEAKS
to the various phases we move through in our love of
country, similarly has my relationship with Mark evolved
and constantly changed. Throughout our twelve years to-
gether we have learned to adapt to each other's needs and
reevaluate our relationship through various life-changing
circumstances. Being named inaugural poet was certainly
one of those circumstances! We've always alternated
roles as primary breadwinners and work-at-home house-
husbands. When we moved to Maine, I had assumed the
latter role, managing our home while also working part-
time on consulting engineering projects. But the intense
pressure of a three-week deadline to finish the inaugural
poems forced me to write every available minute of the
day, well into the morning hours, and consumed all my
mental and physical energy. Mark took over my role and
day-to-day routine: picking up mail at the post office, walk-
ing and feeding Joey, grocery shopping, stoking the fire—
and more. He also took a leave of absence from work so he

could step in as my manager, fielding phone calls, scheduling interviews, and coordinating social media and logistics with the inaugural committee. All so I could write—and write I did, right through Christmas and New Year's Eve.

Mark has always been my first reader, though—that didn't change. I have always valued his input as one of the most intelligent people I know—an accomplished research scientist in his own right. But he's not steeped in the world of poetry and so maintains an important perspective as a reader. His everyday-person's perspective was especially important when I considered the inaugural poem's audience—people from all walks of life with a basic understanding of poetry for the most part. Every night I'd leave him drafts I had finished before going to bed, and the next morning, while I was still sleeping, he would carefully read over them. I'd wake up to giant mushy stars and heart-shaped *I love you*'s scribbled in the margin, which secretly meant as much to me as his brilliant comments and suggestions on the poem that we'd then discuss at length over coffee. I had always been his emotional rock; now he was mine. Support, devotion, encouragement—all these fall under the umbrella of love, which allowed me to keep writing and working even harder.

. . . sometimes praising a mother

who knew how to give . . .

I COULDN'T SAY A WORD ABOUT MY SELECTION FOR
three weeks, until the inaugural committee issued a
press release with the official news. Finally I could tell
my mother! She immediately began making travel plans
with my brother to travel to Washington. However, I was
told that only one guest could be seated next to me on the
platform at the inauguration, which presumably would be
Mark. But he insisted that my mother be the one instead of
him: *The bigger story is about you and your mother—the Amer-
ican Dream*, he told me. *She should be the one with you. I'll be
okay.* It was perhaps the kindest act of selfless love I have
ever received from him. Though I know I would have done
the same had the shoe been on the other foot. I would've
given up my seat for Mark's mother, Carol, who also came
to the inauguration. She is as loving, strong, and caring a
woman as my own mother.

Since the day I met her and the rest of Mark's family,
I felt right at home. Despite our cultural dissimilarities
(they are of Polish, German, and French Canadian de-

scent), I read in them an immigrant story and values quite similar to those of my own Cuban family. For generations, they worked hard and struggled but not at the expense of loving and supporting their children. Mark's parents (and their parents) believed in creating opportunities for their children to have a *better life*. His grandparents had worked in a factory, allowing Mark's parents to graduate high school and move up to white-collar jobs, which allowed Mark to complete doctoral studies in experimental oncology and toxicology and become an honorary fellow at Harvard's Dana Farber Cancer Center, as well as the youngest research scientist ever hired at Pfizer before 1993. Though on the surface our families are obviously very different culturally (my mother is embarrassed to speak English, and Mark and his parents don't speak a word of Spanish), we all speak the same unspoken language of a story familiar to all of us—a story of immigration, struggle, and triumph.

Naturally, Mark understood the reverence and awe my brother, Carlos, and I had for our mother and her courage when she left Cuba, leaving behind her mother, her brother and five sisters, and all her relatives—every uncle and aunt, niece and nephew—never knowing if she'd see them again. *Could I leave America forever?* I asked myself, reflecting on my mother's life and all her losses. This question birthed another of the three poems, "Mother Country," in which I place myself (and the reader) in my mother's emotional shoes, examining the incredible depth of the human spirit and our capacity to survive loss as seen through her eyes. I began taking inventory of all *I* would lose if I had to leave America: I'd never again drive down the gravelly street where I learned to ride my bike or pick a bucketful of loquats from the tree my grandmother and I planted in our backyard, now thirty years tall; never sink my feet along the shore of Miami Beach or hear the waves replying to wishes I've spoken to the sea since I was a child playing in the sand; never again see my brother or step into the secrets we kept and bets we made in the bedroom we shared for twelve years. Or never again sit at the kitchen table of my home in Bethel, where I wrote these words and poems.

I couldn't imagine having to leave my mother, forever. She's always been my emotional center and my connection to Cuba. But in "Mother Country," she also connected me to America in an unexpected way. I realized her story wasn't solely about loss and courage but was also about faith—the incredible faith she must have had in America, which was little more than a set of abstract ideals she had never lived. It occurred to me how strongly immigrants uphold America to those ideals of freedom, justice, and equality, which they do not take for granted. There's the irony that immigrants like my mother stand among the most patriotic of Americans and at the heart of the American Dream. She will sit next to me on the platform of the Capitol. She won't fully understand the poem I will read about America to America in English, but she doesn't have to. She is the poem; she is America.

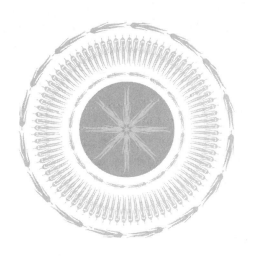

MADRE PATRIA

Amar a un país como si perdieras otro: 1968
mi madre deja Cuba y emigra a los Estados Unidos,
una escena que me imagino, parado en sus zapatos:
un pie dentro del avión camino a un país que sólo
conocía de nombre, un color en un mapa, fotos brillosas
en las revistas de la farmacia. Su otro pie anclado
a la plataforma de su patria, su mano aferrada
a una maleta, solamente con lo más necesario:
fotos de su familia coloreadas a mano,
su velo de novia, el pomo de la puerta de su casa,
un frasco con tierra de su jardín, cartas de despedida
que no abriría en años. El zumbido afligido
de los motores, una última, profunda inhalación, aire
familiar que se lleva con ella, una última mirada a todo
lo que ha conocido: las palmeras se despiden
mientras ella se sube al avión, las montañas se encogen
ante sus ojos, mientras ella despega rumbo a otra vida.

MOTHER COUNTRY

To love a country as if you've lost one: 1968,
my mother leaves Cuba for America, a scene
I imagine as if standing in her place—one foot
inside a plane destined for a country she knew
only as a name, a color on a map, or glossy photos
from drugstore magazines, her other foot anchored
to the platform of her *patria*, her hand clutched
around one suitcase, taking only what she needs
most: hand-colored photographs of her family,
her wedding veil, the doorknob of her house,
a jar of dirt from her backyard, goodbye letters
she won't open for years. The sorrowful drone
of engines, one last, deep breath of familiar air
she'll take with her, one last glimpse at all
she'd ever known: the palm trees wave goodbye
as she steps onto the plane, the mountains shrink
from her eyes as she lifts off into another life.

Amar a un país como si perdieras otro: La escucho
—*érase una vez*—leer libros infantiles en mi cama,
a la hora de dormir, mientras los dos aprendemos
inglés, pronunciando palabras tan extrañas como el habla
de los animales y de las princesas rubias en las páginas.
Pruebo sus primeros intentos de *macaroni-n-cheese*
(pero con chorizo y ají), y su vergüenza por los pavos
siempre secos del día de acción de gracias, pero
contrarrestados con su pernil perfecto y yuca con mojito.
Huelo la lluvia de aquellas mañanas, acurrucados debajo
del paraguas esperando al autobús hacia sus días de diez horas
en la caja registradora. En la noche, el zzz-zzz mientras cose
sus propias blusas, vestidos de quinceañera para las sobrinas
que siguen en Cuba, adivinando sus tallas, y los trajes
que vendía a los vecinos, ahorrando para un sedán blanco
oxidado—sin tapacubos, sin aire acondicionado, sudando
todo el camino de nuestra primera vacación
a los parques de atracciones de Florida.

Amar a un país como si perdieras otro: Como si
estuvieras en un avión que se va de los Estados Unidos
para siempre, y las nubes se cerraran como cortinas sobre *tu* país;
la última escena en la que haces garabatos como loco
de los nombres de tus flores, árboles, y pájaros favoritos
que jamás volverás a ver, tu teléfono y dirección
que jamás volverás a usar, el color de los ojos de tu padre,
el pelo de tu madre, aterrorizado de olvidarlos.
Amar un país como si yo fuera mi madre aquella primavera:
cojeando, insiste que la ayude a subir hasta
el Capitolio. Como si ella fuera yo, aquí hoy

To love a country as if you've lost one: I hear her
—*once upon a time*—reading picture books
over my shoulder at bedtime, both of us learning
English, sounding out words as strange as the talking
animals and fair-haired princesses in their pages.
I taste her first attempts at macaroni-n-cheese
(but with chorizo and peppers), and her shame
over Thanksgiving turkeys always dry, but countered
by her perfect pork *pernil* and garlic *yuca*. I smell
the rain of those mornings huddled as one under
one umbrella waiting for the bus to her ten-hour days
at the cash register. At night, the zzz-zzz of her sewing
her own blouses, *quinceañera* dresses for her grown nieces
still in Cuba, guessing at their sizes, and the gowns
she'd sell to neighbors to save for a rusty white sedan—
no hubcaps, no air-conditioning, sweating all the way
through our first vacation to Florida theme parks.

To love a country as if you've lost one: as if
it were *you* on a plane departing from America
forever, clouds closing like curtains on your country,
the last scene in which you're a madman scribbling
the names of your favorite flowers, trees, and birds
you'd never see again, your address and phone number
you'd never use again, the color of your father's eyes,
your mother's hair, terrified you could forget these.
To love a country as if I was my mother last spring
hobbling, insisting I help her climb all the way up
to the Capitol, as if she were here before you today

frente a ustedes con sus lágrimas y mejillas rosas
como las flores de cerezo que coloreaban el aire
ese día en que se paró, volteó y me dijo:
Sabes, mijo, no importa dónde naces, sino
dónde escoges morir: esa es tu patria.

instead of me, explaining her tears, cheeks pink
as the cherry blossoms coloring the air that day when
she stopped, turned to me, and said: You know, *mijo*,
it isn't where you're born that matters, it's where
you choose to die—that's your country.

Thank the work of our hands . . .

"MOTHER COUNTRY" WAS THE LAST OF THE THREE poems I wrote for the inauguration. I finished it a week after I had completed the first two poems ("What We Know of Country" and "One Today") and submitted them to the inaugural committee and the White House for consideration. Of those two, they had overwhelmingly selected "One Today" as the poem to be read. But once I completed "Mother Country," it became my favorite poem; it was closest to me emotionally, and I felt more comfortable with it because it was the kind of poem I was used to writing. I felt my voice came through more naturally than in the other two poems. And so I submitted "Mother Country" for consideration, but "One Today" remained the preferred poem by the committee and the White House.

Disappointed, I wormholed into a creative turmoil for a couple of days, wondering if I had any bargaining power to insist that "Mother Country" be the inaugural poem. I reached out to friends and writing colleagues for advice, most of whom felt as torn as I did between "One Today" and "Mother Country," mostly because they were such different poems that it was hard to judge. Apples to oranges.

Mark felt that "One Today" was the more appropriate poem from the very first draft, and his instincts would prove to be spot on. But perhaps the biggest champion of "One Today" was writer Julia Alvarez. After I shared a first draft with her, she said without reservation that "One Today" was the perfect poem for the occasion of a country coming together, even if it was for that *one* moment at the inauguration. She eased my apprehensions by noting that some of the best poems in history use the kind of oracular voice she heard in "One Today," a voice that captures the zeitgeist of a moment. Her brilliant advice saved me from going into a tailspin. I also shared the first draft with my former professor and mentor, Campbell McGrath, who agreed for similar reasons with Julia that it was the "right" poem.

In the end, all these conversations and feedback gave me the courage and confidence to move forward with "One Today" and also confirmed what I intuitively had not wanted to admit to myself about "Mother Country": it was too autobiographical for an occasional poem. Though it was a good poem and fit the spirit of the occasion, it didn't fit the purpose of the inauguration as well as "One Today." Also, I realized that for years I had subconsciously believed my work had been well received mostly because of my subject matter as a child of exiles, focused on issues of cultural identity, displacement, and a proverbial search for home.

But I discovered that it wasn't *what* I wrote about but *how* I wrote about it that made my poems *my* poems, namely, the density of imagery and lushness of language that are signatures of my work. Once that clicked, I knew the task at hand was to revise "One Today" along those lines, not by virtue of altering the subject matter but by infusing it with those same qualities and breathing my voice into it. And—as Sandra Cisneros advised—it was important that I approach the poem with the same loving tone as if I *were* speaking about (or to) my mother.

I returned to the first draft of "One Today," ready to work on it with renewed enthusiasm and vigor. But by then I only had one week to turn in the final version, which I'd have to read to hundreds of thousands of people and millions more watching on TV all over the world! Like many poets, I usually put poems away for weeks, months, sometimes years before returning to them. The distance allows for fresh perspective, new insights, and renewed inspiration. But without the luxury of that distance and time, my critical skills became clouded. It became difficult to distinguish exactly what was working from what was not working in the poem, difficult to make editorial decisions with the same ease and confidence that I usually do when not under such intense pressure.

There is a popular misconception that poetry—perhaps all art—happens out of sheer genius or inspiration, and that all artists work alone. That hasn't been my experience. Most writers I know rely on someone they can trust with their work, which essentially implies someone we can also trust with our lives. Luckily, I found both a long time ago in Nikki Moustaki, a brilliant author and poet in her own right, and also my best friend for more than twenty years. I reached out to her, as I have many times before, needing her input more than ever given the circumstances. *Here are some suggestions,* she wrote after reading my first draft of the poem. *Take these in the spirit in which they are intended, with love and wanting you to be YOU.* We dove into discussions about the poem through e-mails and telephone calls that drifted well into the early hours. My editorial skills resurfaced and my confidence grew as I looked over the poem, fine-tuning its images and metaphors, pruning language, and scrutinizing every line, word, and sound. Working together through several drafts of "One Today," it dawned on me that our teamwork was itself a reflection of the poem's very message of unity and togetherness.

All of us as vital as the one light

we move through . . .

*W*HAT DO I LOVE ABOUT AMERICA? THAT WAS the question that eventually yielded the very first draft of "One Today." My initial answer was simply, *The spirit of its people*. And I had begun writing the poem on that impulse, trusting that it and the creative process would lead me to discover something magical. Indeed, much of the creative process happens unconsciously, and I'm always amazed by the way unconscious feelings surface in poems, leading to a new or refined understanding of ourselves. How they always seem to teach me something about myself and my world that I hadn't really acknowledged before. And how they often affect the reader in the same way. During the revision process, as I took a microscopic view of the poem, I began to uncover the many conscious and subconscious experiences—past and present—that had influenced and informed its images, themes, and construction.

Most significant, I discovered that the inspiration for "One Today" harkened back to the story I was born into: the story of the close-knit community of Cuban exiles

that instilled in me a deep sense of mutual respect, compassion, and oneness. I remembered my brother and me
spending almost every weekend with our parents' *haciendo
visitas*—visiting relatives and their old friends from Cuba,
especially the elderly or less fortunate than us who had
just emigrated. My mother would show up with a homemade flan or a home-sewn blouse, sometimes a garbage
bag full of toys or clothes my brother and I had outgrown,
and sometimes just a can of Cuban coffee she had found on
sale. My father would bring his tool box, ready to replace a
leaky faucet, install a new door lock, or fix a broken chair.

And there were those who helped us: When we emigrated from Spain to New York City, my *tía* Olga and *tío*
Armando had already set up an apartment for us in their
building with two months' rent prepaid and a job for my
father working at a bomb factory. Three months and four
days after we arrived in the United States, my father wrote
a letter in his poor English thanking the welfare and social
services departments for their help and letting them know
we would no longer be needing assistance. I stole a carboncopy of that letter from my mother's keepsake box; it's now
one of *my* treasured mementos. Every now and then, when
I am organizing my office closet or riffling through it looking for something I've lost, I find the letter and am struck
again by my parents' courage and dignity.

The same spirit of my exile community was rekindled
when Mark and I moved nearly five years ago to Bethel,
Maine, a small rural town of about 2,500 residents. I had
expected to become enchanted by its quaintness—and I
did. But more so, I was charmed by its townspeople, who,
from the start, went out of their way to make *the two gay*

guys from Miami (as we were known affectionately) feel welcomed—albeit in the most polite and reserved manner typical of New Englanders. Apple pies and housewarming gifts appeared on our porch from Cheri, our real estate agent; Pok Sun inducted us into the coveted chopstick club at her Korean restaurant; Susan and Mike made sure we didn't miss a single summer barbeque or dinner party in town. Perhaps I was still clinging to that television-brand America, but as months turned into years, I began to feel right at home in Bethel, fulfilled by the simple pleasures of walking down our Main Street and waving hello to friends with a smile, spending fifteen minutes talking (and gossiping) in the post office, or running into friends at a restaurant and putting tables together to break bread.

When the news of my selection was made public on January 8, Bethel lived up to my small-town ideal. Jewel, a yodeling champ and folk artist extraordinaire, sweetened our lives with homemade macaroons. Holly gave Mark and me free "make-overs" and began selling copies of my books at her beauty salon. Julie eased our stress with free massages. The proprietors of the Bethel Inn, Mame and Allen, set up a room free of charge for my interviews with National Public Radio and the *New York Times*. Mark's business partners at the lab told him to take off all the time he needed to help me, and his office assistants (Tara, Bailey, Willow, and Sarah) also helped with phone calls and all sorts of miscellaneous tasks. All this generosity let Mark continue managing logistics, freeing up my time to keep working on "One Today." In fact, it was living proof of the central themes of unity and support that had taken root in the poem. Flash forward to my homecoming celebration, organized by the community on my forty-fifth birthday: a six-foot-long cake, a reading at the auditorium with six hundred attendees, a lifetime ski pass, and the naming of a ski run after "One Today."

In Miami there was a similar outpouring. I received dozens of heartwarming messages of congratulations from proud friends, relatives, former professors, and engineering coworkers. My mother's neighbors thought she had won the lottery when the news vans swarmed her house. Suddenly my baby pictures and photos of our family vacations, birthday parties, and weddings flashed on every news channel, as well as interviews of my mother and brother telling our story. A wave of nostalgia came over me, even as I continued working on "One Today." I wanted to hop on a flight and return to the city where most of my life had unfolded: childhood summers with my grandparents in South Beach amid the then-crumbling Art Deco hotels; years later, the nights of my youth at those same hotels, renovated into nightclubs where I learned to dance salsa; the countless number of stops for shots of Cuban coffee and guava pastelitos at cafeterías dotting every street of the city, the same streets and neighborhoods I renovated as an engineer. Flash forward to my Miami homecoming: 1,400 people in attendance at the Arsht Center of the Performing Arts for my poetry reading, where I was presented with the keys to the city and a proclamation marking February 22 as Richard Blanco Day in Miami-Dade County.

Clad with pines or flanked by palm trees, edged by snow-capped mountains or sea-green shores, Bethel and the Miami I grew up in are similar communities in heart and spirit. Miami was the city of my story, and Bethel was the American counterpart of the story I had been foolishly searching for on old TV sitcoms. There was a real America after all, just not the one I had imagined. Although worlds apart, both my nostalgic memories of *my* Miami and *my* present-day Bethel came together through the writing of "One Today." I realized that both communities held several essential things in common for me: respect for the importance of each individual, compassion for one another, and, most important, a deep, abiding sense of dignity and unity.

My poetic sensibilities understood these as the most endearing and enduring qualities of the American spirit. "One Today" became an extension of those values and fundamental beliefs that I wished America to reconnect with as a nation-village, especially in light of so much strife and political division in recent years. In my mind, the purpose of being the inaugural poet and of my poem was to transcend politics and envision a new relationship between all Americans. I wanted America to embrace itself, so to speak, and recognize—no, feel—how we are all an essential part of one whole, if only for those few minutes when I would stand at the podium. Finally I grasped the underlying tension I had been searching for in the poem: namely, the wishing for, the striving for the ideal of being or becoming one, not just for a day, but every day. I came to understand the poem as a kind of prayer, an invocation, with an appeal to our higher selves at its emotional center.

. . . equations to solve, history to question,

or atoms imagined . . .

MANY OTHER ARTISTIC REVELATIONS AND DECI-
sions happened while sitting with America at my
kitchen table in Bethel working on the poem, sometimes
until dawn. In fact, the very first line, *One sun rose on us
today . . .* , struck me as I gazed out the kitchen window,
watching the sun brushing the tips of the hemlocks that
buttress my house. It was the same sun of forty years be-
fore, when I had wanted to believe it was no bigger than a
sunflower; the same sun peek-a-booing through the palm
trees in Miami since I was a child; the same sun my soul
had taken in countless times rising over the ocean. *One sun*
prompted the images of *one sky, one wind, one ground*, and
one moon. These became the armature of "One Today," tap-
ping into the transcendent power of nature as a common
human denominator that connects all our individual sto-
ries. One of the great challenges of writing an occasional
poem is how to be intimate and conversational while also
being grand and Whitmanesque. The natural imagery
became a stand-in for the grandness of the poem, in con-

trast to the intimate details of real people going about their daily lives. The poem began to alternate, breathe, zoom in and out between these two modes.

Another challenge that emerged was establishing the poem's boundaries: Was it possible to have a poem that harkened back to the landing of the Pilgrims and moved forward through hundreds of years of history? No, I decided, thinking such a poem would be too diluted or else it would have to be a two-hundred-page epic. I made a conscious choice to keep the focus of "One Today" on a contemporary setting—a snapshot of the country at our present moment, of which I was a part.

This triggered yet another challenge: how to make the poem *mine*, that is, how to invest myself personally and be vulnerable in the poem, rather than appear distant and preachy? This is why I decided to include specific autobiographical references to my mother and father, and also a moment when I refer to myself as the *living* poet behind the *voice* of the poem, all with the intention of creating an honest, emotional bond between the audience, the poem, and me, making their stories, my story, our story. This same intent prompted me to also include more subtle nods in the poem relating to my life as an engineer, as a gay man, and as a Latino.

In the end, there was no doubt in my mind that "One Today" was the perfect choice for an inaugural poem, one I could proudly read about and for America. Meeting my deadline, January 14, 2013, at noon, I e-mailed the final version of "One Today" to the inaugural committee. They forwarded it to the White House for final review and approval. Surprisingly, within an hour I heard back from the committee with news that the White House had signed off on my final submission with the words *They love it*. I wasn't asked to change a single word or comma. This delighted me, of course, especially thinking that perhaps President Obama himself had read and approved the poem. Was it he who *loved it*?

Regardless, "One Today" was done. For the first time in over a month I was able to take a deep breath and rest. To recharge, I returned to my regular small-town routine for a few days: taking Joey for long walks in the park, catching up on gossip at the post office and grocery store, and getting together for dinner to celebrate with friends—finally.

. . . as these words break from my lips

B UT THERE WAS ONE MORE VERY IMPORTANT THING
left to do: practice the delivery of the poem. Surpris-
ingly, the inaugural committee didn't coach me in any way
or ask me to recite the poem for them beforehand. They
completely trusted me, but I knew I had to practice—and I
did in a most unusual and unexpected way.

A few weeks prior to the inauguration, my brother and
nephews had visited us during the holidays and made a
snowman that was still "alive" in the field below our deck.
One morning I woke up to find Mark on the deck setting
my reading folder and a photo of President Obama atop
a makeshift podium he fashioned out of a cardboard box.
Read to the snowman, he insisted. *You should rehearse outside.
Feel what it's going to feel like.*

At first I thought it was a silly idea and that perhaps
Mark was cracking under the stress. But then it occurred
to me that at the inauguration I would indeed have to read
into an immense open space before hundreds of thousands.
It *would* be a good idea to envision that moment and get a

sense of reading outdoors, especially in the cold. If I could handle the Maine winter with ten-degree highs, surely DC wouldn't be a problem. *One sun rose on us today* . . . I began, feeling the stare of the snowman's stony eyes—he was a tough audience! I shifted my gaze toward the sun—my sunflower—afloat over the Presidential Range (how ironic) of the White Mountains in the distance. I spoke into the wind breezing through the pine trees, aimed my words up to the blank blue sky, and heard them fall over the ground frozen with all its surprises for spring, as if standing inside the very poem I had written when the first blush of the moon's face appeared.

My greatest fear, of course, was that I'd stumble over the words while I was at the podium. So I memorized the poem during the days before we left for Washington. Like a madman, I read it out loud in the shower and while driving into town, mumbled it to myself while jogging on the treadmill and walking down the grocery store aisles. More than merely memorizing, I was rehearsing the poem's performance as if it were a song to be sung, internalizing it physiologically: the timing of my breaths, the cadences, the sound of each syllable, until the poem was embodied in me. Poetry was born in the oral tradition, something I have always strived to honor, believing that reciting a poem should create an experience for the listener unique from that of simply reading the poem on the page.

The delivery of "One Today" was especially important as a poem that would be heard before it would ever be read. I had about five minutes—one chance—to captivate Americans and connect with them. As such, I continued to revise the poem like a musician, reworking phrases that sounded off-key or felt too convoluted for the ear, marking dramatic pauses and underlining words like notes I wanted to hold.

After rehearsing the poem for about a week, I knew it was time to put it away, let it rest for a while, and trust it as I trusted that the snow would melt even as I watched it fall outside my window that January. Believe in it as much as I believed the bulbs Mark had planted would break through the wet earth into pink and yellow tulips come spring.

. . . alongside us, on our way . . .

M ARK AND I HAD LIVED IN WASHINGTON, DC,
for over three years, from 2001 to 2004, so the
city was still somewhat familiar when we arrived. This
was comforting in no small way, but even more comfort-
ing was the *village* that traveled to the capital with me and
had been with me emotionally and spiritually since I first
received the news. Mark arranged for us to all stay in the
same hotel: my good friend Nikki, acting as my social-
media guru; Alison Granucci, my agent from Blue Flower
Arts speakers' agency and also a kind of godmother, offer-
ing spirited words and joining me in impromptu dances
in my hotel room; Meredith Beattie, a natural-born leader
with a rare combination of chutzpah and love, representing
City Year, a national school-mentorship program I planned
to partner with; my cousin Sergio Baradat, a brilliant art-
ist who would design the cover and interior illustrations
for this book, as well as an elegant broadside of the poem;
David Naranjo, my publicist, who offered his expertise

and energy to help us navigate the media frenzy; and, of course, my mother, brother, and mother-in-law.

When we arrived, the city was abuzz with inauguration activity. There were souvenir vendors all over the National Mall and special inauguration-themed menus and drinks being served at restaurants; details about the ceremony and festivities appeared on every news program. Even as I saw my name flashed across the TV screens in the lobby of our hotel—"Richard Blanco, Inaugural Poet"—I hadn't quite fathomed the entire scope of such an honor. For the most part, poets live and write contentedly inside the circle of literati and academics, myself included. Accustomed to that kind of relative obscurity, I naively thought I'd simply read my poem, shake a few hands, get back home, and that would be that. Not so. The days ahead proved to be abruptly life changing, filled with unexpected experiences and realizations that were somewhat tangential to the writing of the poem but nevertheless important and unique parts of my journey as inaugural poet.

Ushered around by David, I spent the first few days in the city with my village dashing from one interview to another at major news stations from the United States and around the world (CNN, Telemundo, the BBC, Univision, PBS). Suddenly I was thrust into a whole new world of make-up rooms, microphone wires, spotlights, and newsroom sets, with cameras eyeing me from every angle. It was terrifying and yet wonderful, thanks to David, who dissipated my anxiety with his witty one-liners that kept me in stitches. But more important, he was a *cubanito* like me, who grew up in my Miami. He knew my story, wanted me to tell it, and believed in it. He empowered me to trust that my story was important and to believe it could make a difference in the lives of millions of immigrants and LGBT people—all of them Americans. I soon felt and accepted a responsibility to speak so that we might all be heard, respected, and legitimized. The sense of serving a greater good, afforded by my role as inaugural poet, was humbling and gave me the courage to look into the cameras honestly and speak the most intimate details of my life to the world without reservation.

But David hadn't expected *a poet* to step into the spotlight as naturally as I did. Even I was surprised by how comfortable I began to feel in front of the cameras. In retrospect, I understand that something grander took over my being, rooted in my personal beliefs about the art of poetry. Throughout years of writing, I had come to think of the poem as a mirror in which the reader and the poet stand side by side: the reader catching a reflection of his or her own life blurred with the poet's life. Connecting to people—and having them connect emotionally to their own lives—had become a kind of personal mission underlying my poems, my fundamental belief that *this* indeed was the ultimate beauty, power, and purpose of poetry. I recognized the inaugural poem as a great opportunity—perhaps the single greatest opportunity I'd have—for poetry to engage America in this way: "One Today," a great big mirror for all of us to look into, together. An even greater sense of purpose and duty as inaugural poet emerged as a result, emboldening me to speak about poetry and my story.

Evenings we attended several pre-inauguration events throughout the city, witnessing an interesting intersection of politics and celebrity—DC meets Hollywood. I must confess I had held a slight aversion toward celebrities and most pop icons, believing poetry and poets had no place in their world. But I was proven wrong. At one dinner party I had a most unexpected conversation with Eva Longoria about Latino literature and her initiative for the Latino Museum in DC. She was also one of the minds behind the Latino Inaugural 2013, a special celebration at the Kennedy Center, where actor Wilmer Valderrama performed a dramatic reading of my poem "When I Was a Little Cuban Boy." Backstage, he told me how much he loved the poem and confessed that he'd been rehearsing it for days, wanting to get it *just right*. I had similar exchanges about poetry and literature with almost every celebrity and mover-and-shaker I met, from Star Jones to the mayor of San Antonio, Julian Castro, from will.i.am to Nancy Pelosi. Everyone seemed genuinely interested in my story, proud of my selection as poet, and excited about poetry, often asking me for a hint about what my inaugural poem was about. The inauguration had poetry on everyone's minds, I realized, demonstrating its potential to hold a more vital, popular place in our lives, even in the lives of celebrities.

. . . this poem for us today. All of us . . .

THE NIGHT BEFORE THE INAUGURATION, I PRAC-
tice reading the poem aloud one last time in my hotel
room, imagining four hundred thousand snowmen listen-
ing to me. I then sit quietly by myself, marking up my read-
ing copy and preparing my binder with the poem. In the
sleeve I put a hand-colored photo of my maternal grand-
parents, whom I had never met, wanting them to be with
me in spirit at the podium. I look into the story in their eyes
again, my mother's story, my story. And I also place one of
Mark's notes that I'd saved in which he wrote: READ IT/
FEEL IT. LOSE YOURSELF IN THE POEM. A certain peace
falls over me and I doze off with the poem cradled in my
hands, held against my chest. Mark eventually wakes me
up. I stumble to bed and fall back asleep knowing my life
will never be the same after tomorrow. I don't remember
what I dreamt that night, but it wouldn't have mattered:
the line between dream and reality had blurred almost be-
yond recognition. My life, the poem, and the moment are
one by then.

I'm not a morning person, but on January 21, I'm up and about at 6:30 a.m., wanting to savor the day that will only happen once in my lifetime. After three double espressos, I take the poem out yet again and find a solitary spot outside on the lower terrace of the hotel. For the last time I begin reading over it silently: *One sun rose on us today* . . . And as I do, the sun begins peeking above the rooftops as if enacting the poem, blinding me the way Robert Frost was blinded by the sun the morning of his inaugural reading decades ago. I'm not one to readily believe in mystical signs, but if there ever is a time to believe something greater is speaking to me, it is now. The sun becomes a sunflower—my sunflower again; for a moment it again revolves around the earth, around me and the poem in my hands.

I get dressed, put on the silver eagle cufflinks that Mark surprised me with as a gift the day before. I then straighten my tie and catch my eyes in the mirror. But they are not my eyes, exactly; they are the eyes of the poet who will read. It is that familiar, though infrequent, feeling that many artists speak of, that sense of being a channel, a medium possessed by the muse. By 8:30 a.m. I find myself riding in a motorcade just like in the movies, darting through the streets in a black SUV with my mother and Mark seated beside me, along with David, Nikki, and Alison. Just as we did during the sound-check rehearsal, we are escorted by staff into one of the Capitol offices—the holding room. We can barely speak, keeping a reverent silence as we wait, our eyes glued to the TV monitor panning scenes of the inaugural stage, where my mother and I will soon take our seats. A few minutes before being called out, we gather in a circle and hold hands in a prayer led by David to offer our gratitude for the beauty of the moment unfolding before us.

Arm in arm, I escort my mother down the steps to the Capitol platform. Her story began when she was born in a dirt-floor home in rural Cuba. She sold oranges to pay for schoolbooks and had only one pair of shoes, and now she is a guest of honor seated next to her son on stage with the president of the United States, members of the US Congress and Supreme Court, as well as James Taylor, Kelly Clarkson, and Beyoncé. I'm not sure if my mother was nervous, proud, bored, shocked, or all of the above. She's always been a hard person to read. Sometimes she comes across as fearless and blunt (*When they going to start dis thing? I'm freezing,* she complains). Other times vulnerable (she takes my hand and tells me, *Ay mijo, I wish tu padre could be here with us*), sometimes animated and jovial *(I used to have a figure como la Beyoncé, believe it or not,* she claims, cracking a smile), other times stoic and reserved. She gives me that wide-eyed look I've known since I was a child, silently telling me to sit still, behave, stop fidgeting with my binder, which I flip through over and over again to make sure all the pages of the poem are there. I adjust my tie a half dozen times and glance at my wristwatch every few minutes. My mother offers me a honey-filled candy. A mother no matter the occasion—my mother, beside me as she has always been, with a piece of candy, a scolding, a kiss, a complaint, or a story to tell me.

The horns blare and the ceremony finally begins. I begin taking it all in, listening to the opening remarks by Senator Charles Schumer, followed by Myrlie Evers-Williams's invocation. Slowly and unexpectedly, a powerful feeling of innocent pride for my country takes over. Something I hadn't felt since grade-school days coloring dittos of the Pilgrims and Indians at Thanksgiving, or George Washington chopping down the cherry tree, or maps of the fifty states. Since I first memorized the Pledge of Allegiance and "The Star-Spangled Banner." Or the first time I read the Declaration of Independence in high school. Instead of becoming increasingly nervous as my time at the podium approaches, I become entranced by a palpable sense of reverence and unity. I am struck by the importance of the occasion, together with the hundreds of thousands of people—*we*—who have come to bear witness to the founding ideals of America, which come to life during the inauguration; we, who have come to remind our elected president, *You are here because we are here.*

In the moment I feel America standing as one, putting differences aside, and taking a deep collective breath. We pay tribute to something far bigger and more important than any one of us. And I truly feel like one of *us*, one of *We, the people*, in the echoes of the president's inaugural speech:

> We, the people, declare today that the most evident of truths—that all of us are created equal—is the star that guides us still; just as it guided our forebears through Seneca Falls, and Selma, and Stonewall; just as it guided all those men and women, sung and unsung, who left footprints along this great Mall, to hear a preacher say that we cannot

walk alone; to hear a King proclaim that our individual freedom is inextricably bound to the freedom of every soul on Earth.

I embrace America in a way I never had or thought I could, feeling for the first time that I belong—truly belong—to *one* country. Not an imaginary ideal from TV or a nostalgic island floating in the sea of my parents' memories, but a real, tangible place that is mine—was mine all along. I turn to my mother and whisper, *"Mamá*, I think we're finally *americanos."* She gives me a tender look as if saying, *I know, I know.* Indeed, I realize it was always *one* story I was born into, *one* story for me to discover and claim, *one* story to make my own.

In that instant I understand "One Today" as a gift to America. Inspired by that realization, I find the courage to open up my binder to the poem and add "for us today" at the end of the second stanza, as well as tinker with a few other phrases. Again I am struck by the trust the administration has placed in me; I could have read a radically different poem than the one they had read and selected.

Senator Charles Schumer introduces me and calls me up to the podium. My mother squeezes my shoulder. I stand more confident than I imagined I would or could be, transfixed by the moment that is no longer about me, or *my* poem, or *my* glory, but about *our* America. Still, I'm surprised when the president and vice president stand up to greet me and shake my hand on my way to the podium; they both whisper something in my ear that I can't make out. But their gracious gestures speak silently to my heart, as if saying: *Here is your country. This is your story.* I step up to the podium, look out over the crowd: a patchwork quilt of lives, of stories spread across *our* ground, under *our* sky, beneath *our* one sun. I take it all in as I take one deep breath, then another. *This is for them, for us, for all of us,* I think to myself and begin speaking into *our* wind: "Mr. President, Mr. Vice President, America . . ."

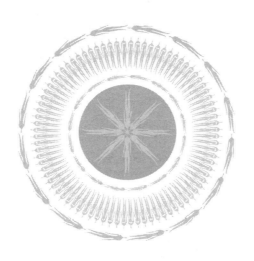

HOY, UNO

Un mismo sol hoy, encendido sobre nuestras costas,
se asoma sobre las Smokies, saluda las caras
de los Grandes Lagos, difunde una simple verdad
a través de las Grandes Llanuras, luego a la carga por las Rocosas.
Una misma luz despierta los techos: debajo de cada uno, un cuento
de nuestros gestos que se mueven, callados, detrás de las ventanas.

Mi rostro, tu rostro, millones en los espejos de la mañana,
cada uno bostezando a la vida, culminando en nuestro día:
camiones de escuela amarillo lápiz, el ritmo de los semáforos,
puestos de fruta: manzanas, limones, y naranjas surtidos como
    arcoíris
suplican nuestros elogios. Carreteras rebosando de camiones plata
cargados con aceite o papel, ladrillos o leche, junto a nosotros.
Vamos de camino a limpiar mesas, a leer registros o a salvar
    vidas—
a enseñar geometría, o atender la caja registradora como lo hizo
    mi madre
durante veinte años, para que yo pudiera escribirles este poema hoy.

ONE TODAY

One sun rose on us today, kindled over our shores,
peeking over the Smokies, greeting the faces
of the Great Lakes, spreading a simple truth
across the Great Plains, then charging across the Rockies.
One light, waking up rooftops, under each one, a story
told by our silent gestures moving behind windows.

My face, your face, millions of faces in morning's mirrors,
each one yawning to life, crescendoing into our day:
pencil-yellow school buses, the rhythm of traffic lights,
fruit stands: apples, limes, and oranges arrayed like rainbows
begging our praise. Silver trucks heavy with oil or paper—
bricks or milk, teeming over highways alongside us,
on our way to clean tables, read ledgers, or save lives—
to teach geometry, or ring up groceries as my mother did
for twenty years, so I could write this poem for us today.

Cada uno de nosotros tan vital como la luz única que atravesamos
la misma luz en los pizarrones con las lecciones del día:
ecuaciones por resolver, historia por cuestionar, o átomos
    imaginados,
el "Yo tengo un sueño" que seguimos soñando,
o el vocabulario imposible de la tristeza que no explica
los pupitres vacíos de veinte niños ausentes
hoy, y para siempre. Muchas plegarias pero una misma luz
inhala color a los vitrales,
sopla vida a las caras de las estatuas, y calienta
los escalones de nuestros museos y bancas del parque
mientras las madres observan a los niños adentrarse en el día.

Una misma tierra. Nuestra tierra, nos arraiga a cada tallo
de maíz, a cada espiga de trigo sembrados con sudor
y manos, manos que cosechan carbón o plantan molinos de viento
en los desiertos y las colinas para darnos calor, manos
que cavan zanjas, trazan tuberías y cables, manos
tan gastadas como las de mi padre que cortaban caña
para que mi hermano y yo tuviéramos libros y zapatos.

El polvo de nuestras granjas y desiertos, ciudades y planicies
mezclado por un mismo viento—nuestro aliento. Respira.
    Escúchalo
en el hermoso estruendo del día: los taxis y su claxon,
autobuses disparados por las avenidas, la sinfonía
de los pasos, guitarras y el chirrido del metro,
el inesperado pájaro cantor en tu tendedero.

All of us as vital as the one light we move through,
the same light on blackboards with lessons for the day:
equations to solve, history to question, or atoms imagined,
the "I have a dream" we keep dreaming,
or the impossible vocabulary of sorrow that won't explain
the empty desks of twenty children marked absent
today, and forever. Many prayers, but one light
breathing color into stained glass windows,
life into the faces of bronze statues, warmth
onto the steps of our museums and park benches
as mothers watch children slide into the day.

One ground. Our ground, rooting us to every stalk
of corn, every head of wheat sown by sweat
and hands, hands gleaning coal or planting windmills
in deserts and hilltops that keep us warm, hands
digging trenches, routing pipes and cables, hands
as worn as my father's cutting sugarcane
so my brother and I could have books and shoes.

The dust of our farms and deserts, cities and plains
mingled by one wind—our breath. Breathe. Hear it
through the day's gorgeous din of honking cabs,
buses launching down avenues, the symphony
of footsteps, guitars, and screeching subways,
the unexpected song bird on your clothes line.

Escucha: columpios chillones, trenes que silban,
o murmullos en los cafés. Escucha: las puertas
que abrimos todo el día: *hello* / *shalom* /
buon giorno / *howdy* / *namaste* / o *buenos días*
en el idioma que mi madre me enseñó—en todos los idiomas
hablados al mismo viento que lleva nuestras vidas sin
prejuicio, mientras estas palabras parten de mis labios.

Un mismo cielo: desde que los Apalaches y las Sierras reclamaron
su majestad, y el Misisipí y el Colorado labraron
su camino hasta el mar. Agradece el trabajo de nuestras manos:
que tejen el hierro en puentes, terminan un reporte más
para el jefe, cosen otra herida o uniforme, la primer pincelada
de un retrato, el último piso de la Torre de la Libertad
resaltado en un cielo que cede ante nuestra resiliencia.

El mismo cielo hacia el cual a veces levantamos la mirada,
cansados de trabajar: unos días adivinamos el clima
de nuestra vida, otros días agradecemos un amor
que nos ama de vuelta, unas veces alabamos a una madre
que supo darnos más que todo, otras veces perdonamos
a un padre que no pudo dar lo que queríamos.

Volvemos a casa: a través del brillo de la lluvia, o el peso
de la nieve, o el rubor del atardecer, pero siempre, siempre
a casa, siempre debajo de ese cielo, nuestro cielo. Y siempre
una misma luna como tambor callado golpeteando en todos los
	techos
y en cada ventana de un país—todos nosotros—
de cara a las estrellas. *La esperanza*—una nueva constelación aguarda
que la tracemos, aguarda que la nombremos—juntos.

Hear: squeaky playground swings, trains whistling,
or whispers across café tables. Hear: the doors we open
for each other all day, saying: *hello / shalom /
buon giorno / howdy / namaste / or buenos días*
in the language my mother taught me—in every language
spoken into one wind carrying our lives
without prejudice, as these words break from my lips.

One sky: since the Appalachians and *Sierras* claimed
their majesty, and the Mississippi and *Colorado* worked
their way to the sea. Thank the work of our hands:
weaving steel into bridges, finishing one more report
for the boss on time, stitching another wound
or uniform, the first brush stroke on a portrait,
or the last floor on the Freedom Tower
jutting into a sky that yields to our resilience.

One sky, toward which we sometimes lift our eyes
tired from work: some days guessing at the weather
of our lives, some days giving thanks for a love
that loves you back, sometimes praising a mother
who knew how to give, or forgiving a father
who couldn't give what you wanted.

We head home: through the gloss of rain or weight
of snow, or the plum blush of dusk, but always, always
home, always under one sky, our sky. And always
one moon like a silent drum tapping on every rooftop
and every window, of one country—all of us—
facing the stars. *Hope*—a new constellation waiting
for us to map it, waiting for us to name it—together.

When I finish, there is dead silence, and for a moment I think, *Well, I better not quit my day job yet.* Later I will realize this is because of the sound delay. But a second or two after I turn from the podium, I hear applause and cheers from the crowd behind me, while facing a standing ovation from those on the platform, including the president and vice president, who shake my hand again.

As I make my way back down the aisle, I scan smiles of approval and eyes filled with a reverent glee. Associate Justice Sonia Sotomayor gives me a nod. James Taylor reaches into the aisle, touches my arm, and whispers, *Great job, man.* Despite the praise, I'm overwhelmed by the magnitude of the moment, caught in a complexity of emotions: feeling a great sense of accomplishment and yet simply grateful that I didn't trip over the steps or my words; filled with pride and yet bashful from all the attention; anxious about how the poem went over and yet perfectly at ease knowing that I had done my very best and given the assignment—and my country—all I had to give.

. . . *all of us—facing the stars*

O N MY WAY TO THE HOLDING ROOM, I SEE ALISON
wanting to skip down the hall and do a cartwheel—
I can tell from the glee in her eyes. Without saying a word,
she embraces me, and I pick her up, spin her through
the air in my arms. Back in the room, I and my village
of highly educated and respected professionals, who had
worked so hard and seamlessly, know we've earned the
right to celebrate unabashedly and get just plain silly in a
private moment belonging to us, solely to us. Intoxicated
with joy (and relief), we bounce around the room that
can hardly contain our jubilation, hugging each other and
making toasts with orange juice and water bottles. David
wraps his scarf around me and we break into a conga step.
Nikki darts around the room reporting the tweets coming
in: "Oh my god, you're trending worldwide! Oh my god,
you're ahead of Beyoncé!" All this being caught by Mark,
snapping a photo every three seconds, recording the eter-
nal moment being born inside us. My mother, in a stoic
loss for words, asks me where the bathroom is, and in the

same breath tells me she loves me and asks me to sit with her for a moment.

We spill back into the hall buzzing with people, where we meet Myrlie Evers-Williams, Rev. Dr. Luis León, James Taylor, Kelly Clarkson—all of us in electrified celebration. There are more handshakes, hugs, and mutual words of congratulations and praise. Then we hear from Beyoncé's entourage that she wants to meet *the poet*, and we are escorted into her holding room. She tells me how much she enjoyed the poem. I thank her, compliment her on her performance, and ask, "Were you as nervous as I was?" thinking that surely a superstar such as she wouldn't be. But she was, she says, and tells me that at least she was singing someone else's song; she couldn't imagine what it must have been like for me to read something I wrote myself. Beyoncé is gracious and genuine, and to answer the question I will get asked dozens of times: *Yes*, she *is* just as beautiful in person.

Mark and I are bused to the official presidential grandstand, where I soon after meet the vice president's brother, Frank Biden, waiting in line for hot chocolate. He shares with me that my poem was *the talk* of the afternoon luncheon with the president and Congress. The woman tending the hot-chocolate stand overhears us. *Oh you're the poet*, she smiles and shares the story of her mother—an immigrant like my mother—who came from the Ukraine and worked in a factory in New York City into her seventies. Others at the parade introduce themselves and offer congratulations. Some say it was the best moment of the inauguration for them. I am flattered by everyone's comments and responses, but it's a much more complex feeling, difficult to explain exactly. A kind of mutual gratitude, a moment shared in one joy of simultaneous giving and receiving.

After the parade, as Mark and I walk through the streets trying to find our designated shuttle bus back to the hotel, people begin recognizing me as *the poet*. They stop me, share snippets of their responses to the poem: *I felt like part of America for real. . . . It was as if you were speaking to me. . . . It made me cry. . . . Thank you, thank you*. We take pictures together, they tell me about their lives, their stories. Some are teachers, firemen, lawyers; other are secretaries, accountants, housekeepers—the same people that live in "One Today," I realize. They ask how they can get copies of the poem for their children, students, grandmothers, and neighbors. A petite Asian-American woman darts out of an alley, kisses me, and insists I sign her copy of the inaugural program. A ten-foot-tall doorman grabs me in a bear hug and says, *Come here—give me some love, brother.* I had wanted to embrace America through "One Today"; I wanted Americans to embrace each other. But I hadn't expected that America would embrace me and that the poem would be gifted back to me in such a way.

Mark and I become completely disoriented; we have no idea how to get back to the hotel. Most of the streets are closed; there are no cabs in sight, and we have about an hour to get ready for the inaugural ball. A woman— an angel—appears on a corner. She stares at me in amazement, as if she has been looking for me, and says, *I knew I would find you.* She hugs me and introduces herself as Lara, a psychologist and writer. After we explain our predicament, she says, *Well, I got a car—I'll give you a ride.* We climb into her Toyota, her golden retriever Rusty growling at Mark in the back seat. On the way to the hotel we talk about Einstein, quantum physics, love, the source of creativity, and "One Today," as if we have known each other all our lives. I promise to try to get her into the inaugural ball, but I never see the angel again.

Similar interludes and exchanges continue through the hotel lobby and in the elevator. In the hall on the way to our room I take pictures with some of the housekeeping staff, and we begin chatting in Spanish. I ask them where they are from and they ask me where I am from, which suddenly feels like a whole different question to me after the inauguration. Mark pulls me into the room; we shower, change into our tuxedoes in twenty minutes, then meet the others in the lobby and head to the inaugural ball in a caravan of taxis.

I had thought I was going to have a ball at the ball, maybe even get a chance to dance with the First Lady or have a quiet moment with the president to ask him what he thought of the poem and how I was selected. Not so. Soon after we arrive, I realize the grand scale of the inaugural ball: thousands of people from all over the country and the world. Not an intimate setting, but an intimate feeling nevertheless. Despite the fact that most are strangers to each other, there's a sense of belonging to each other, a common motive for celebration, a oneness, much like at the inauguration, much like the poem.

Before the president arrives, and I realize I won't meet him, we dash to the CNN studios for an interview with Anderson Cooper, whom I had long admired for his work and courage for leading an openly gay life. I'm a little starstruck when we meet, but he is the same person as he appears on television: gracious, friendly, genuinely intrigued—and a great interviewer who makes me feel at ease, as if I'm simply chatting in his living room. From the CNN studios we rush off to the Human Rights Campaign ball. The organizers had told everyone I wasn't going to attend; they had wanted my appearance to be a surprise, and it is, for me as well: I walk onstage to say a few words, but I'm silenced by three minutes of whistles, applause, and hollers. Though I have lived an openly gay life for decades, I came of age in a generation fraught with homophobia. As such, I think there was still some small part of me that hadn't fully accepted myself as a gay man until that very moment when I am overcome by the crowd's response, the palpable love from *my* LGBT community. Not a town or a city but a home nevertheless, where I belong as much as I belong to America.

. . . a new constellation . . .

MORE INTERVIEWS ARE SCHEDULED FOR EARLY
the next morning. We call it a night, and my vil-
lage reconvenes in my hotel room. We slip off our shoes,
brew some tea, and begin a round-robin reading of the
thousands of e-mails and Facebook messages we received
throughout the day and which are still coming in. Mes-
sages from senior citizens and schoolchildren, from for-
eign nationals and New Englanders who were alive to see
Frost read his poem, from gay and straight soldiers and par-
ents, from prominent Latinos and those as salt-of-the-earth
as my mother and father, from members of Congress and
immigrant families from all over the globe. The messages
are like poems. They speak of their tears and hand holding
as they listened to the poem, their sense of belonging and
healing, their pride and hope, their lives and *Americanness*.
As a poet, I've been schooled to never conjure up clichéd
imagery, but there is no other way to say this: we stumble
over words blurred by our tears, at times our voices sur-

render to silence as the only fitting homage to the pure, uncensored honesty we feel unworthy to read aloud.

Throughout the next day, before leaving Washington, I continue living and breathing these messages. They reconfirm my belief in poetry as a mirror, able to affect and enhance lives, but they also call to mind my long-held concerns about the state of poetry in America. *Why isn't poetry a part of our cultural lives and conversations; part of our popular folklore as with film, music, and novels?* I suddenly remember my first trip to Cuba, when I tell my cousins and uncles that I'm a poet, and they take out their guitars, a bottle of moonshine rum, and ask me to "sing with them." I don't understand what they mean. They begin strumming and singing to the moon in Spanish through impromptu *décimas*, a syllabic and rhymed poetic form. Most of my relatives have a high school education at best, and yet they know poetry; they know their national poets and can quote verses from Nicolás Guillén, José Lezama Lima, and José Martí, who to this day is considered a Cuban national hero referred to as the "Apostle." Poetry is entrenched in their history, rooted in their folklore, established in their national identity and their very lives.

Reflecting back on my own life, I realize that all throughout grade school, high school, and college I was never introduced to a single poem by a living poet. Unacceptable. Not until I began taking creative writing courses on my own after college did I encounter the incredible spectrum of contemporary poets writing about the very communities and issues of my day. Poetry then became alive and relevant to my life. Why hadn't that happened sooner?

I think of all the middle school children I've worked with over the years, how their eyes light up when we read and discuss poetry that mirrors their own families, neighborhoods, lives, and experiences.

The messages from my country speak clearly to me of the great potential and hope for poetry in America. In a visionary moment, I know the greater good that must come from my honor as inaugural poet. I make a conscious commitment to keep connecting America with poetry and reshape how we think about it, to try to dispel the myths and misconceptions about the art by introducing us to more contemporary work that speaks to our lives in *real time*. And, moreover, to explore how I can empower educators to teach contemporary poetry and foster a new generation of poetry readers. I think again about Sandy Hook, those children who died, but also those children and parents who survived them. I know there is poetry that can help them process their grief, make sense of the senseless, find a way to heal, and believe the sun is a sunflower again.

. . . waiting for us to map it . . .

to name it—together

NESTLED IN OUR SEATS AT THE AIRPORT, MARK and I wait to board our flight back home. We're still electrified but too exhausted to even speak. All we can do is quietly watch the mass of people herding through the terminal: businessmen in suits clutching their iPads or military men in uniform lugging their duffle bags, women in pantsuits or mothers pushing their strollers, everyone in the act of leaving or returning, in the mystic flux of journey. The public-address system sounds like an oracle, announcing flights, calling out passenger names and their destinations. And it all feels strangely familiar, old yet new, sharp yet dull, bright yet muted, like those few minutes some mornings in bed with half my life still in a dream and the other half of me being born anew into the miracle of yet another morning. The end of one story inexplicably transitioning into another.

It's the first opportunity I have to truly sit quietly for a moment and reflect on the whole experience of the inauguration with a little distance. I'm again struck with a *know-*

ing that nothing will ever be the same, though I'm not sure what those changes and experiences will be or how they will indeed prove to me that poetry can have a place and power in our contemporary lives, like no other art form.

It's about thirty minutes before our departure time. I don't know that in a few months I will interview with the editors of the *Newtowner*, an arts and literature magazine from Newtown, Connecticut. We will plan classroom visits and a special event on the anniversary of the Sandy Hook tragedy to bring the community together in poetry and healing, as I had wanted to do since the day it happened, since the day I penned "One Today" to remember those children forever. I don't know of the thousands of people who will stir my soul through letters I will receive, each one sharing a life changed by their reflection in "One Today" or my other poems, enthused by a rekindled or newfound love for poetry. I don't know that in May I'll meet President Obama in the Oval Office and we will speak about his and the First Lady's ongoing commitment to poetry. I will present the president with Sergio's beautiful broadside of "One Today," which he'll hang in his back office where he'll say he keeps those things closest to him.

The boarding process begins. I get in line, but I don't know of the Boston Marathon bombings, the boy and two young women whose lost lives I'll feel compelled to immortalize in "Boston Strong," an occasional poem I'll write and read before tens of thousands of people at the opening of a concert at Boston's TD Garden to benefit the survivors and victims' families. Imagine, a poem (in America) as an opening act—so to speak—for James Taylor, Jimmy Buffett, Carole King, the Backstreet Boys, Aerosmith, and other artists who will come together for the cause. Imagine poetry being able to make a difference alongside them. A few weeks later I'll read the same poem again in Fenway Park before a Red Sox game: baseball, hot dogs, poetry, and apple pie—why not? I don't know that I will also be asked to write and read another occasional poem for the Tech Museum of Innovation at their annual awards gala in Santa Clara, California. Poetry in Silicon Valley—why not?

I fasten my seatbelt as instructed without knowing that in June the Supreme Court will rule the Defense of Marriage Act unconstitutional in favor of Edith Windsor, and I will team up with the Freedom to Marry organization to write a love poem commemorating a ten-year struggle for marriage equality. I can't imagine a poet—much less me—will be the grand marshal of the gay pride parade in Portland, Maine. I don't know that I will speak at Portland's Immigrant Legal Advocacy Project, read poems and sing "God Bless America" like I never have before alongside Somali and Congolese, whose stories of and love for this country would be as epic as my mother's. I can't fathom that a poet—much less me—will be honored with keys to the cities of Portland, Miami, and Miami Beach. I don't know that I'll again be in the company of celebrities such as Taylor Swift at the Fragrance Foundation Awards in New York's Lincoln Center, where I will read a poem I wrote, "To the Artists of the Invisible," blending the romance of scents with the sense of words. Perfume and poetry—why not?

The plane pushes back from the gate, but I don't know about the grade school and high school teachers from around the country who will send me hundreds of poems, drawings, and letters by their students, inspired and given hope by "One Today." I do not know that I will be asked to read and share my story and poems at a conference of engineers, one of whom will stand up and confess to everyone in the room that he's been writing poetry for years to make sense of his life. As I have. I do not know that after a poetry reading on Cape Cod a woman will embrace me and recite a line from one of my poems (. . . *pretend that nothing lost, is lost*) as tears well up in her eyes because she can't help pretending she hasn't lost the son she'd lost just a few months ago. Nor have I met the woman in Vermont who will tell me she keeps a copy of "One Today" on her kitchen table and reads it on those days she feels she can't go on. I'll tell her poetry is what keeps me going, too. Nor has the elderly man from Buffalo confided in me that he's written into his will that "One Today" be read at his funeral. I'll remember my own wish to have Elizabeth Bishop's "One Art" read when I die.

The plane taxies down the runway without my knowing that in July I'll read my poetry at the Robert Frost farm in Derry, New Hampshire. I will walk through his home, sit in his chair at the kitchen table where he wrote, and feel the ghost of his words at my fingertips as I lay my hands over the typewriter keys. Suddenly I will understand why Frost was *Frost*—arguably our country's most celebrated, honored, popular, and remembered poet—because he wrote about (and for) the things and people right before him, *his* America, plain and true. His work was embedded in folklore, sprung from the very pastures and pleasures, snows and sorrows of the people—including himself—in his own backyard, so to speak. Inspired and possessed, I'll feel reborn into yet another story—the story Frost began for America. I'll feel a responsibility to dare and dream up a new chapter that will rekindle poetry into a continuing American folklore—a folklore that would include the stories of gay America, Latino America, and immigrant America—everyone's America.

The jet's engine begins revving up, and so do I, beginning to think about this memoir that I will write in the months to come: part proclamation, part call to action, but all testimony—not to the power of *me*, or *my* work, or *my* story, but to the power of poetry as I will have witnessed it; to the hunger for poetry in our country; to the powerful role it can play and the influence it can have on so many lives, including my own. I know—believe—there's a new dawn at hand for poetry and for poets as heroes, which parallels a new dawn in America and its changing human landscapes. I know I have work to do. I know I have to get back home—yes, *through the gloss of rain or weight of snow, or the plum blush of dusk*—and begin writing. I know poetry can matter.

Mark looks at me and holds my hand as the plane lifts off the ground, carried on *one* wind, lifting us into *one* sky crisp and bright as grace in my eyes, under our *one* sun. The sun *is* a sunflower after all. I gaze out my window at the Capitol—its radiating columns and arches of concrete ideals resemble a sunflower as we fly above it. Indeed, our country is a sunflower with millions of petals around a center we can't always see or always understand, but one flower nonetheless, one story, the story we are *all* born into. A story we all have to continue writing together until we are not just *one today,* but one *every day.*

I had left Maine with a single poem to offer my country that I didn't quite understand. I returned as an American, driving back home through the pines of Maine under *one* moon but with a thousand more stars and poems for me— for us all—to write, for us.

Acknowledgments

Thank the work of our hands, indeed—and of the minds, hearts, and souls of my village that saw me through this journey and was with me on the ground in Washington, DC: Nikki Moustaki, for her literary genius; Alison Granucci, for her spiritual merrymaking; David Naranjo, for his cultural kinship and joie de vivre; Sergio Baradat, for his images that mirror my soul; Meredith Beattie, for her leadership as even-keeled as her love; Carol Neveu, for being true as my mother; my mother, Geysa, for absolutely everything; my brother, Carlos, for loving his little brother; and my partner, Mark Neveu, the poet behind my poetry. Thanks to my village-in-spirit: Adrienne Landau, Ed Fagin, Deborah Slack, Stephen and Doreen Fishman, Brad and Stacy Standley, Sandra Cisneros, Julia Alvarez, Campbell McGrath, and Natasha Trethewey. Thanks to Miami, my city-village of all those known and unknown from which my poetic voice was born. Thanks to the townspeople of Bethel, who confirmed my belief in the true spirit of America, especially Jewel Clark,

Aranka Matolcsy, Susan Duplessis, Mike DiPhilippo, Jim Doar, Al Cressy, Holly Roberts, Bill and Sue Pike, Mo and Rob Lally, Dana Bullen, the Bethel Inn, Pok Sun Lane, Bailey Davis, Willow Ochtera, Sarah Swan, Tara Lunney, Ed and Amy Yasko—well, the whole blessed town, really! Thanks also to Frank Cimler, who I trusted would make this book possible; hats off to Mitchell Kaplan, whose generous spirit paired me with Beacon Press; and cheers to Helene Atwan, who perfectly understood this story I had to tell.

For their extraordinary support, kindness, and words of praise for this book (which you can read on my website), I want to thank Barnet Bain, Jennifer Benka, Frank Biden, Roger W. Bowen, Michael F. Brennan, Senator Susan Collins, Lorraine Cortes-Vazquez, Timothy Gunn, Aranka Matolcsy, Marilyn Moss-Rockefeller, Congresswoman Chellie Pingree, Tim Ritchie, Liv Rockefeller, Anthony D. Romero, Howard Rosenman, Lisa Schwartz, Anastasia Tonello, and Evan Wolfson.